Buckeyeology
Trivia
Challenge

Ohio State Buckeyes Football

Buckeyeology Trivia Challenge

Ohio State Buckeyes Football

Researched by Tom P. Rippey III

Tom P. Rippey III & Paul F. Wilson, Editors

Kick The Ball, Ltd
Lewis Center, Ohio

Trivia by Kick The Ball, Ltd

COLLEGE FOOTBALL TRIVIA

Alabama Crimson Tide	Georgia Bulldogs	Nebraska Cornhuskers	Oregon Ducks
Auburn Tigers	LSU Tigers	Notre Dame Fighting Irish	Penn State Nittany Lions
Boston College Eagles	Miami Hurricanes	Ohio State Buckeyes	Southern Cal Trojans
Florida Gators	Michigan Wolverines	Oklahoma Sooners	Texas Longhorns

PRO FOOTBALL TRIVIA

Arizona Cardinals	Denver Broncos	Minnesota Vikings	San Francisco 49ers
Buffalo Bills	Green Bay Packers	New England Patriots	Washington Redskins
Chicago Bears	Indianapolis Colts	Oakland Raiders	
Cleveland Browns	Kansas City Chiefs	Pittsburgh Steelers	

PRO BASEBALL TRIVIA

Boston Red Sox	Cincinnati Reds	New York Yankees	Saint Louis Cardinals
Chicago Cubs	Los Angeles Dodgers	Philadelphia Phillies	

COLLEGE BASKETBALL TRIVIA

Duke Blue Devils	Indiana Hoosiers	Kentucky Wildcats	North Carolina Tar Heels
Georgetown Hoyas	Kansas Jayhawks	Michigan State Spartans	UCLA Bruins

PRO BASKETBALL TRIVIA

Boston Celtics	Los Angeles Lakers

Visit **www.TriviaGameBooks.com** for more details.

Dedicated to the biggest Buckeye fan I know, Victor Jones

Buckeyeology Trivia Challenge – Ohio State Buckeyes Football; Fourth Edition 2009

Published by
Kick The Ball, Ltd
8595 Columbus Pike, Suite 197
Lewis Center, OH 43035
www.TriviaGameBooks.com

Designed, Formatted, and Edited by: Tom P. Rippey III & Paul F. Wilson
Researched by: Tom P. Rippey III

For information on ordering this book in bulk at reduced prices, please email us at pfwilson@triviagamebooks.com.

International Standard Book Number: 978-1-934372-59-3

Printed and Bound in the United States of America

10 9 8 7 6 5 4 3 2 1

Table of Contents

BUCKEYEOLOGY TRIVIA CHALLENGE

Dear Friend,

Thank you for purchasing our **Buckeyeology Trivia Challenge** game book!

We have made every attempt to verify the accuracy of the questions and answers contained in this book. However it is still possible that from time to time an error has been made by us or our researchers. In the event you find a question or answer that is questionable or inaccurate, we ask for your understanding and thank you for bringing it to our attention so we may improve future editions of this book. Please email us at tprippey@triviagamebooks.com with those observations and comments.

Have fun playing **Buckeyeology Trivia Challenge**!

Tom and Paul

Tom Rippey and Paul Wilson
Co-Founders, Kick The Ball, Ltd

PS – You can discover more about all of our current trivia game books by visiting www.TriviaGameBooks.com.

How to Play

Book Format:

There are four quarters, each made up of fifty questions. Each quarter's questions have assigned point values. Questions are designed to get progressively more difficult as you proceed through each quarter, as well as through the book itself. Most questions are in a four-option multiple-choice format so that you will at least have a 25% chance of getting a correct answer for some of the more challenging questions.

We've even added an *Overtime* section in the event of a tie, or just in case you want to keep playing a little longer.

Game Options:

One Player -

To play on your own, simply answer each of the questions in all the quarters, and in the overtime section, if you'd like. Use the *Player / Team Score Sheet* to record your answers and the quarter *Answer Keys* to check your answers. Calculate each quarter's points and the total for the game at the bottom of the *Player / Team Score Sheet* to determine your final score.

Two or More Players –

To play with multiple players decide if you will all be competing with each other individually, or if you will form and play as teams. Each player / team will then have its own *Player / Team Score Sheet* to record its answer. You can use the quarter *Answer Keys* to check your answers and to calculate your final scores.

1

The *Player / Team Score Sheets* have been designed so that each team can answer all questions or you can divide the questions up in any combination you would prefer. For example, you may want to alternate questions if two players are playing or answer every third question for three players, etc. In any case, simply record your response to your questions in the corresponding quarter and question number on the *Player / Team Score Sheet*.

A winner will be determined by multiplying the total number of correct answers for each quarter by the point value per quarter, then adding together the final total for all quarters combined. Play the game again and again by alternating the questions that your team is assigned so that you will answer a different set of questions each time you play.

You Create the Game -
There are countless other ways of using **Buckeyeology Trivia Challenge** questions. It is limited only to your imagination. Examples might be using them at your tailgate or other college football related party. Players / Teams who answer questions incorrectly may have to perform a required action, or winners may receive special prizes. Let us know what other games you come up with!

Have fun!

First Quarter

1-Point Questions

1) What year did Ohio State officially adopt the nickname Buckeyes for the school's athletics?

    A) 1920
    B) 1936
    C) 1950
    D) 1969

2) What are the Buckeyes' official colors?

    A) Black and Yellow
    B) Scarlet and White
    C) Orange and Blue
    D) Scarlet and Gray

3) What is the name of the stadium where the Buckeyes play?

    A) Value City Stadium
    B) Cooper Stadium
    C) Ohio Stadium
    D) Woody Hayes Field

4) What year did Ohio State play its first-ever game?

    A) 1890
    B) 1897
    C) 1905
    D) 1912

5) What is one of the most recognizable college football traditions performed by the Ohio State marching band?

A) Alumni Band March
B) Script Ohio
C) Drum line
D) Playing in the stands

6) Who was the Buckeyes' starting quarterback in the 2002 National Championship game?

A) Craig Krenzel
B) Troy Smith
C) Steve Bellasari
D) Joe Germaine

7) In the lyrics of the Ohio State fight song, where will "our cheers" reach?

A) The Field
B) To a Score
C) For Team Victory
D) The Sky

8) Which Buckeyes head coach had the longest tenure?

A) Woody Hayes
B) John Cooper
C) Earl Bruce
D) Paul Brown

9) Who was the first player from Ohio State to be picked number one in the NFL Draft?

- A) Orlando Pace
- B) Archie Griffin
- C) Eddie George
- D) Tom Cousineau

10) How many Heisman Trophies have been won by Ohio State players?

- A) 1
- B) 2
- C) 5
- D) 7

11) What charm do Ohio State players receive after a win against Michigan?

- A) Silver #1
- B) Gold Horseshoe
- C) Gold Pants
- D) Platinum Horseshoe

12) Does Ohio State have an overall winning record against Penn State?

- A) Yes
- B) No

13) What is the name of Ohio State's mascot?

   A) Buster
   B) Stinger
   C) Brutus
   D) Bucky

14) What is the name of the pep rally that takes place in St. John Arena before every Buckeye home game?

   A) Coach Talk
   B) Skull Session
   C) Band Walk
   D) Fan Craze

15) Ohio Stadium has a seating capacity of over 100,000.

   A) True
   B) False

16) In which year was Ohio State's first undefeated season (minimum 8 games)?

   A) 1899
   B) 1912
   C) 1916
   D) 1928

First Quarter

BUCKEYEOLOGY TRIVIA CHALLENGE

17) What is written across Brutus Buckeye's scarlet and gray horizontal-striped shirt?

- A) Buckeyes
- B) Ohio State
- C) OSU
- D) Brutus

18) What famous rock and roll song can fans expect to hear the marching band perform at Ohio State games?

- A) "Rock Around the Clock"
- B) "Hang on Sloopy"
- C) "Wild Thing"
- D) "Jailhouse Rock"

19) Who holds the career rushing record at Ohio State?

- A) Keith Byars
- B) Archie Griffin
- C) Maurice Clarett
- D) Vic Janowicz

20) Who was the Buckeyes' first consensus All-American?

- A) Chris Spielman
- B) Hopalong Cassady
- C) Chic Harley
- D) Warren Amling

21) What was the result of Archie Griffin's first carry as a Buckeye?

     A) Touchdown
     B) Fumble
     C) 6-yard loss
     D) 52-yard gain

22) Senior Tackle traditionally takes place the last practice before which Ohio State game?

     A) Northwestern
     B) Indiana
     C) Penn State
     D) Michigan

23) Which coach has the most wins as a Buckeye?

     A) Jim Tressel
     B) Paul Bixler
     C) Woody Hayes
     D) John Cooper

24) What year did Ohio State join the Big Ten (then known as the Western Conference)?

     A) 1908
     B) 1912
     C) 1918
     D) 1922

25) Who holds the record for passing yards in a single game at Ohio State?

    A) Joe Germaine
    B) Kirk Herbstreit
    C) Rex Kern
    D) Art Schlichter

26) What is the name of the bell that rings to signal every Buckeye win?

    A) Monon Bell
    B) Scoring Bell
    C) Victory Bell
    D) Bell by the Olentangy

27) Which is the only U.S. Service Academy to defeat OSU?

    A) Never lost to a U.S. Service Academy
    B) Army
    C) Navy
    D) Air Force

28) Under which Ohio State coach did the tradition of awarding Buckeye leaves begin?

    A) Earl Bruce
    B) Wes Fessler
    C) Woody Hayes
    D) Alexander Lilly

29) Have Ohio State and Michigan ever played on a neutral site?

    A) Yes
    B) No

30) Who holds the Ohio State record for total yards against Michigan in a single game?

    A) Pete Johnson
    B) Hopalong Cassady
    C) Troy Smith
    D) Bobby Hoying

31) Who led the Buckeyes in sacks in 2008?

    A) Thaddeus Gibson
    B) Cameron Heyward
    C) Marcus Freeman
    D) James Laurinaitis

32) Which team has Ohio State played the most in bowl games?

    A) Notre Dame
    B) UTEP
    C) Southern Cal
    D) UCLA

First Quarter

33) Who received the most individual national awards while at Ohio State?

A) Eddie George
B) Rex Kern
C) Archie Griffin
D) Troy Smith

34) In which of the following categories did Keith Byars not lead the nation in 1984?

A) Scoring
B) Rushing
C) All-purpose yards
D) Receiving

35) Which award did Troy Smith not win in 2006?

A) Maxwell Award
B) Heisman Trophy
C) Davey O'Brian Award
D) Walter Camp Award

36) Who was the first three-time consensus All-American for Ohio State?

A) Mike Nugent
B) Chic Harley
C) A.J. Hawk
D) Cris Carter

First Quarter

37) What is the name of the trophy that is passed to the winner of the Ohio State-Illinois game?

   A) Bucknut Trophy
   B) Illibuck Trophy
   C) Buckilli Trophy
   D) Saginaw Trophy

38) What song does the team sing to fans after every Ohio State game?

   A) "Carmen Ohio"
   B) "Hang on Sloopy"
   C) "America the Beautiful"
   D) "Beautiful Ohio"

39) Who holds the OSU season record for receiving yards?

   A) Terry Glenn
   B) Cris Carter
   C) David Boston
   D) Brian Robiskie

40) What instrument does the band member who dots the "i" play?

   A) Drums
   B) Flute
   C) Trombone
   D) Sousaphone

41) How many AP National Championships has Ohio State been awarded?

    A) 2
    B) 4
    C) 5
    D) 7

42) What is the name of the Ohio State fight song?

    A) "Buckeye Battle Cry"
    B) "Carmen Ohio"
    C) "Victors Today"
    D) "Ohio is Our Home"

43) The Illibuck Trophy is in the shape of what animal?

    A) Dolphin
    B) Turtle
    C) Chimpanzee
    D) Alligator

44) How many Big Ten Championships has Ohio State won?

    A) 18
    B) 24
    C) 33
    D) 38

45) Which player holds the single-game rushing record at Ohio State?

    A) Keith Byars
    B) Eddie George
    C) Robert Smith
    D) Jim Otis

46) Who was the first consensus All-American quarterback for Ohio State?

    A) Les Horvath
    B) Rex Kern
    C) Cornelius Greene
    D) Troy Smith

47) How many OSU head coaches lasted one season or less?

    A) 2
    B) 6
    C) 8
    D) 11

48) What award did Buckeye cornerback Malcolm Jenkins win in 2008?

    A) Jim Thorpe Award
    B) Fred Biletnikoff Award
    C) Vince Lombardi Award
    D) Bronko Nagurski Award

49) Who holds the Ohio State career record for points scored?

- A) Tim Williams
- B) Mike Nugent
- C) Vlade Janekievski
- D) Bob Ferguson

50) Which season did the Buckeyes first celebrate a victory over Michigan?

- A) 1901
- B) 1919
- C) 1923
- D) 1931

First Quarter Buckeye Cool Fact

The University of Michigan marching band actually was the first to perform script Ohio. They performed a script of OHIO diagonally across the field at Ohio Stadium in 1932. The Ohio State marching band would not perform their version of Scrip Ohio until October 10, 1936. The University of Illinois also performed a script of Ohio at Ohio Stadium in 1936 after it had already been performed earlier that day by the Ohio State marching band. The now famous kick, turn, and bow by the "i" dotter was an impulse reaction by sousaphone player Glen Johnson. The drum major arrived at the top of the "i" too soon, so Johnson improvised to take up the additional time. The kick, turn, and bow instantly became a hit, becoming a part of the performance ever since.

First Quarter Answer Key

1) C – 1950 (The name Buckeyes became widely associated with Ohioans since William Harrison adopted the tree as a campaign symbol in 1840.)

2) D – Scarlet and Gray (Adopted by the school in 1878)

3) C – Ohio Stadium (The stadium opened in 1922 with a construction cost of $1.3 million and original capacity of 66,210.)

4) A – 1890 (The game took place at Ohio Wesleyan with the Buckeyes coming away with a 20-14 victory.)

5) B – Script Ohio (The Ohio State marching band first performed it at home in 1936 against Pittsburgh.)

6) A – Craig Krenzel (He led the Buckeyes to a 31-24 victory over the Miami Hurricanes.)

7) D – The Sky ("…And when the ball goes over, Our cheers will reach the sky…")

8) A – Woody Hayes (28 years, 1951-78)

9) D – Tom Cousineau (A linebacker, he was picked number one overall in 1979 by the Buffalo Bills.)

10) D – 7 (Les Horvath [1944], Vic Janowicz [1950], Hopalong Cassady [1955], Archie Griffin [1974 and 1975], Eddie George [1995], and Troy Smith [2006])

11) C – Gold Pants (This tradition started in 1934 after Coach Francis Schmidt mentioned that Michigan players "put their pants on one leg at a time just like everybody else." Under Coach Schmidt, the Buckeyes went on to outscore Michigan 114-0 his first four years from 1934-37.)

12) A – Yes (The Buckeyes are 12-11 against the Nittany Lions for a .522 winning percentage.)

13) C – Brutus (He first appeared in 1965. His name was chosen through a contest.)

14) B – Skull Session (Initially started as a last band rehearsal, it has grown into an honored pre-game pep rally that begins two hours before kickoff, including a walk through by the players and Coach Tressel.)

15) A – True (Current capacity is 102,329 giving Ohio State the fourth largest on-campus stadium in the country.)

16) A – 1899 (Ohio State went 9-0-1 in their tenth season.)

17) D – Brutus (Written in white upper case letters across one of the shirt's red stripes)

18) B – "Hang on Sloopy" (First played by the Ohio State marching band in 1965 versus Illinois.)

19) B – Archie Griffin (He rushed for 5,589 yards from 1972-75.)

20) C – Chic Harley (He was named All-American in 1916 after leading the Buckeyes to a 7-0 record.)

21) B – Fumble (Most people remember Archie's spectacular game against North Carolina in 1972 where he set a then Ohio State single-game rushing record with 239 yards. However, Archie's first career carry was in the previous game against Iowa and resulted in fumble.)

22) D – Michigan (This tradition began in 1913.)

23) C – Woody Hayes (He led the Buckeyes to 205 wins from 1951-78.)

24) B – 1912 (Ohio State did not begin conference play until 1913.)

25) D – Art Schlichter (Art completed 31-52 passes for 458 yards against Florida State in 1981 [OSU 27, FSU 36].)

26) C – Victory Bell (Donated by the classes of 1943-45, the bell was first rung to celebrate a Buckeye victory over California in 1954 [OSU 21, Cal 13].)

27) D – Air Force (The Buckeyes only loss to a U.S. Service Academy was to the Falcons in the 1990 Liberty Bowl [OSU 11, Air Force 23].)

28) C – Woody Hayes (Awarding Buckeye leaves was actually the idea of team trainer Ernie Biggs. The decals have been given to reward team, unit, and individual accomplishments since 1968.)

29) B – No (The game has always been played at Ohio State or Michigan.)

30) C – Troy Smith (Troy gained 386 total yards against the Wolverines in 2004 [18 rushes for 145 yards and one TD; 13 of 23 passes for 241 yards and two TDs]. He also had 337 total yards in 2005 and 328 total yards in 2006 leading the Buckeyes to three straight wins against the Wolverines.)

31) A – Thaddeus Gibson (He led the team with five sacks for -27 yards.)

32) C – Southern Cal (Ohio State played the Trojans a total of 7 times [3-4] in the Rose Bowl, most recently in 1985.)

33) C – Archie Griffin (Five total awards: Heisman and Walter Camp in 1974; Heisman, Maxwell, and Walter Camp in 1975)

34) D – Receiving (Keith Byars led the nation in the following categories in 1984: rushing [1,655 yards], all-purpose yards [2,284 yards], and points scored [144 points].)

35) A – Maxwell Award (This award was given to Notre Dame Quarterback Brady Quinn.)

36) B – Chic Harley (1916-17, 1919)

37) B – Illibuck Trophy (This tradition began in 1925. Members of honorary societies from each school meet at halftime to pass the trophy to the previous year's winner. OSU leads the Illibuck series 57-23-2.)

38) A – "Carmen Ohio" (Coach Tressel started the tradition in 2001. Players sing to fans in the south stands at home and to the OSU section at away games.)

39) C – David Boston (In 1998, Boston had 85 receptions for 1,435 yards and 13 touchdowns.)

40) D – Sousaphone (One requirement to dot the "i" is to have been a band member for four years.)

41) B – 4 (1942, 1954, 1968, and 2002)

42) A – "Buckeye Battle Cry" (Written by *Ohio* graduate Frank Crumit in 1919, the song is played during the band's entrance onto the field and during Script Ohio.)

43) B – Turtle (Initially a live turtle was used, but was replaced with a wooden turtle in 1927. Since then, there have been a total of 9 wooden turtles used.)

44) C – 33 (The most recent one was in 2008.)

45) B – Eddie George (Eddie had 36 carries for 314 yards and 3 touchdowns against Illinois in 1995 [OSU 41, Illinois 3].)

46) D – Troy Smith (He was named All-American in 2006 after leading the Buckeyes to the National Championship game.)

47) B – 6 (Charles Hickey [1896], David Edwards [1897], Howard Jones [1910], Harry Vaughn [1911], John Richards [1912], and Paul Bixler [1946])

48) A – Jim Thorpe Award (Jenkins led the Buckeyes with nine pass break-ups and three interceptions on the season. The Thorpe Award is given to the nation's best defensive back according to the Jim Thorpe Association.)

49) B – Mike Nugent (Nugent scored a total of 356 points from 2001-04 [140 extra points and 72 FGs].)

50) B – 1919 (After compiling a 0-13-2 record against the Wolverines, the Buckeyes got their first win at Michigan [OSU 13, MICH 3].)

Note: All answers valid as of the end of the 2008 season, unless otherwise indicated in the question itself.

Second Quarter *2-Point Questions*

1) What shaped letter does the student body make in the south stands of Ohio Stadium?

    A) Block O
    B) Little h
    C) Big B for "Bucks"
    D) Big S for "Student Section"

2) What number did Archie Griffin wear while at OSU?

    A) 25
    B) 32
    C) 42
    D) 45

3) How many OSU defensive players are in the College Football Hall of Fame?

    A) 1
    B) 3
    C) 5
    D) 7

4) How many different decades have the Buckeyes won at least 85 games?

    A) 0
    B) 2
    C) 3
    D) 4

5) Has any other team played in more BCS National Championship games than Ohio State?

    A) Yes
    B) No

6) How many times has Ohio State finished a season undefeated?

    A) 3
    B) 5
    C) 6
    D) 9

7) When was the first time the Buckeyes traveled out of state for a game?

    A) 1895
    B) 1899
    C) 1903
    D) 1907

8) Which U.S. Service Academy has Ohio State never played?

    A) Air Force
    B) Navy
    C) Army
    D) Has played all three

Second Quarter *2-Point Questions*

9) Archie Griffin is the only college football player to win two Heisman Trophies.

    A) True
    B) False

10) Which school has Ohio State played fewer than 75 times?

    A) Michigan
    B) Illinois
    C) Indiana
    D) Wisconsin

11) What is Ohio State's all-time winning percentage against Michigan?

    A) .429
    B) .468
    C) .497
    D) .528

12) Who holds the Ohio State record for most passing yards in a single game against Michigan?

    A) Mike Tomczak
    B) Joe Germaine
    C) Jim Karsatos
    D) Craig Krenzel

13) How many times has Ohio State hosted ESPN's
College GameDay?

    A) 9
    B) 11
    C) 13
    D) 17

14) What year was OSU's first-ever winning season?

    A) 1892
    B) 1899
    C) 1902
    D) 1908

15) What is the record for most points scored by Ohio State
against Michigan?

    A) 35
    B) 42
    C) 50
    D) 63

16) Which Ohio State quarterback holds the Big Ten career
passing efficiency record?

    A) Bobby Hoying
    B) Greg Fry
    C) Kirk Herbstreit
    D) Troy Smith

Second Quarter *2-Point Questions*

17) How many times have the Buckeyes scored 50 or more points in a game?

 A) 67
 B) 70
 C) 82
 D) 91

18) What is the longest winning streak in the Ohio State-Michigan series?

 A) 5 games
 B) 7 games
 C) 9 games
 D) 11 games

19) How many Ohio State players have been picked number one overall in the NFL Draft?

 A) 1
 B) 3
 C) 4
 D) 6

20) The Buckeyes have won greater than 20 bowl games.

 A) True
 B) False

21) How many yards was the longest rushing play in Ohio State history?

- A) 76
- B) 82
- C) 89
- D) 99

22) In which bowl was OSU's first-ever bowl appearance?

- A) Cotton Bowl
- B) Rose Bowl
- C) Insight.com Bowl
- D) Blue Bonnet Bowl

23) Who is the only Ohio State player to be named a Rhodes Scholar?

- A) Mike Lanese
- B) Craig Krenzel
- C) Bobby Hoying
- D) Randy Gradishar

24) How many times has Ohio State appeared in the Rose Bowl?

- A) 5
- B) 9
- C) 11
- D) 13

25) Did Ohio State pass for greater than 2,500 yards as a team in 2008?

    A) Yes
    B) No

26) What year did Ohio State win its first Big Ten title?

    A) 1913
    B) 1916
    C) 1919
    D) 1922

27) How many times has Ohio State started the season number one in the first AP Poll?

    A) 2
    B) 4
    C) 7
    D) 9

28) Who is the only Ohio State player to be twice awarded a bowl's MVP?

    A) Craig Krenzel
    B) Keith Byars
    C) Troy Smith
    D) Carlos Snow

29) Who was Ohio State's head coach in its first season of football?

A) Perry Hale
B) Red Grange
C) Alexander Lilly
D) Charles Widdoes

30) Did Terrelle Pryor lead the Big Ten in passing efficiency in 2008?

A) Yes
B) No

31) Who owns the Ohio State record for most receiving yards in a single game against Michigan?

A) Bobby Olive
B) Terry Glenn
C) Joey Galloway
D) David Boston

32) Against which BCS conference does Ohio State have the best winning percentage?

A) Big 12
B) SEC
C) Pac-10
D) ACC

Second Quarter *2-Point Questions*

33) Has a Buckeye rushed for 200 or more yards in a single game against Michigan?

    A) Yes
    B) No

34) Which year was the first conference game between Ohio State and Michigan?

    A) 1913
    B) 1918
    C) 1920
    D) 1924

35) To which team did Ohio State suffer its worst loss in its first season?

    A) Kenyon
    B) Denison
    C) Ohio Wesleyan
    D) Wooster

36) Who was Ohio State's first opponent in Ohio Stadium?

    A) Illinois
    B) Toledo
    C) Ohio Wesleyan
    D) Indiana

37) In which of the following categories did Eddie George lead the nation in 1995?

A) Receptions
B) Fumbles
C) Scoring
D) Rushing

38) How many three-time consensus All-Americans does Ohio State have?

A) 1
B) 3
C) 5
D) 7

39) Who holds the Ohio State record for passing yards in a season?

A) Steve Bellisari
B) Tom Tupa
C) Joe Germaine
D) Art Schlichter

40) Ohio State is the only Big Ten school to have a quarterback win the Heisman Trophy.

A) True
B) False

Second Quarter *2-Point Questions*

41) Who holds the OSU single game receiving yards record?

  A) Santonio Holmes
  B) Terry Glenn
  C) Ken-Yon Rambo
  D) Gary Williams

42) How many Buckeyes have had over 1,000 yards receiving in a single season?

  A) 2
  B) 4
  C) 5
  D) 7

43) Who was the first consensus All-American defensive back at Ohio State?

  A) Jack Tatum
  B) Mike Doss
  C) Damon Moore
  D) Mike Sensibaugh

44) How many outright Big Ten Championships has Ohio State won?

  A) 11
  B) 14
  C) 17
  D) 19

Second Quarter *2-Point Questions*

45) What two jersey numbers did Ohio State retire in 2001?

A) 27 and 47
B) 40 and 31
C) 22 and 27
D) 45 and 47

46) Which Ohio State record did Robert Smith break in 1990?

A) Freshman rushing record
B) Single game rushing record
C) Running back receiving record
D) Running back reception record

47) Who was the last player to wear number 47 for Ohio State?

A) Chic Harley
B) Pepper Johnson
C) Bobby Carpenter
D) A.J. Hawk

48) How many times has Coach Tressel won National Coach of the Year in his career?

A) 0
B) 1
C) 3
D) 4

49) What decade did Ohio State have the best winning percentage?

    A)   1940s
    B)   1960s
    C)   1970s
    D)   1990s

50) Who is the only non-QB from Ohio State to win the Rose Bowl MVP?

    A)   David Boston
    B)   Mike Vrabel
    C)   Fred Morrison
    D)   Archie Griffin

Second Quarter Buckeye Cool Fact

Buckeye fans have been singing along to "Hang on Sloopy" since 1965. Fan response was tepid the first time it was played by the band during a game. This may have been partially due to the heavy rain falling that day. Fans went crazy, however, when the song was played at the next game. It has been synonymous with Ohio State ever since. Due to the fans' seismic response when the song was played, university officials requested that the band not play the song during the game against Syracuse in 1988 until the structural integrity of the press box had been tested. It had been noted on various occasions that the press box would shake during the playing of the song. The State of Ohio's General Assembly made "Hang on Sloopy" the official rock song of Ohio in 1985, making Ohio the first state to have an official rock song. The first playing of the song by the Ohio State marching band is referenced in the resolution.

Second Quarter Answer Key

1) A – Block O (Formed by the largest on-campus
        organization, Block O, which first began in 1938.)

2) D – 45 (His was the first number to be retired in 1999.
        Andy Katzenmoyer was the last player to wear this
        number [1996-98].)

3) B – 3 (Warren Amling was inducted in 1984 as a
        defensive tackle, Randy Gradishar was inducted in
        1998 as a linebacker, and Jack Tatum was
        inducted in 2004 as a safety.)

4) C – 3 (The Buckeyes had 91 wins in the 1970s, 91 wins
        in the 1990s, and have recorded 91 wins in the
        2000s.)

5) A – Yes (Ohio State has played in three BCS title games
        [2002, 2006, and 2007]. Oklahoma has played in a
        total of four BCS title games.)

6) D – 9 (Five seasons with no losses or ties [1916, 1944,
        1954, 1968, and 2002], and four seasons with no
        losses and one tie [1899, 1917, 1961, and 1973].)

7) A – 1895 (The Buckeyes' first out-of-state road game
        was an 8-6 victory at Kentucky seven games into
        the season.)

8) C – Army (The Buckeyes are 3-1 all time versus the U.S.
        Service Academies [0-1 versus Air Force and 3-0
        versus Navy].)

9) A – True (Though many players have won the trophy as underclassmen, Archie is the only player to win the trophy twice.)

10) D – Wisconsin (OSU has played the Badgers 74 times [Michigan 105, Illinois 95, and Indiana 82 times].)

11) A – .429 (Ohio State's overall record against Michigan is 42-57-6.)

12) B – Joe Germaine (1998, 16-28 for 330 yards)

13) B – 11 (ESPN's *College GameDay* began visiting college campuses in 1993. The last appearance at OSU was when the Buckeyes played Penn State in 2008.)

14) A – 1892 (The Buckeyes went 5-3 their third season.)

15) C – 50 (1961 [OSU 50, MICH 20] and 1968 [OSU 50, MICH 14])

16) D – Troy Smith (Troy holds the Big Ten record with a 153.0 career passing efficiency.)

17) B – 70 (OSU is undefeated when scoring 50+.)

18) C – 9 games (Michigan won each year from 1901-08.)

19) B – 3 (Tom Cousineau in 1979 to Buffalo, Dan Wilkinson in 1994 to Cincinnati, and Orlando Pace in 1997 to St. Louis)

20) B – False (The Buckeyes have a record of 18-22 in bowl games for a .450 winning percentage.)

21) C – 89 (Gene Fekete had an 89-yard run against Pittsburgh in 1942, but failed to score.)

22) B – Rose Bowl (The Buckeyes played the Cal Bears in the 1921 Rose Bowl [OSU 0, Cal 28].)

23) A – Mike Lanese (He was named a Rhodes Scholar in 1985 and is the last Big Ten player to be recognized as such.)

24) D – 13 (1921, 1950, 1955, 1958, 1969, 1971, 1973-76, 1980, 1985, and 1997)

25) B – No (OSU quarterbacks completed 160 of 267 passes for 1,953 yards, 17 TDs, and 6 INTs.)

26) B – 1916 (The Buckeyes finished 4-0 in conference play outgaining Big Ten opponents 90-29.)

27) C – 7 (1942, 1958, 1969, 1970, 1980, 1998, and 2006)

28) A – Craig Krenzel (He was named MVP of the 2003 and 2004 Fiesta Bowls.)

29) C – Alexander Lilly (He led OSU to a 1-3 record the first season.)

30) A – Yes (He had an overall rating of 146.5. Second on the list was Daryll Clark of Penn State with a rating of 143.44.)

31) D – David Boston (1998, 10 receptions for 217 yards)

32) A – Big 12 (The Buckeyes are 28-5-1 against Big 12 teams for a .838 winning percentage.)

33) A – Yes (Chris "Beanie" Wells rushed for 222 yards on 39 carries for two touchdowns in 2007, making him the only Buckeye to rush for over 200 yards against the Wolverines.)

34) B – 1918 (Ohio State started league play in 1913 and Michigan rejoined the conference in 1918.)

35) D – Wooster (Ohio State fell 0-64 to the Fighting Scots.)

36) C – Ohio Wesleyan (OSU beat the Battling Bishops 5-0 in Ohio Stadium's inaugural game on Oct. 7, 1922.)

37) C – Scoring (George scored a total of 152 points.)

38) B – 3 (Chic Harley [1916-17, 1919], Wes Fesler [1928-30], and James Laurinaitis [2006-08])

39) C – Joe Germaine (Joe completed 230-384 [.599] for 3,330 yards in 1998.)

40) A – True (Les Horvath [1944] and Troy Smith [2006] are the only Big Ten quarterbacks to win the Heisman trophy.)

41) B – Terry Glenn (He gained 253 yards on 9 receptions against Pittsburgh in 1995 [OSU 54, Pitt 14].)

42) B – 4 (Cris Carter [1,127 yards in 1986], Terry Glenn [1,411 yards in 1995], David Boston [1,435 yards in 1998], and Michael Jenkins [1,076 yards in 2002])

43) A – Jack Tatum (He was named All-American as a defensive back in 1969 and 1970.)

44) C – 17 (The last one was in 2007.)

45) C – 22 and 27 (The then first and last Heisman trophy winners [Les Horvath and Eddie George] respectively.)

46) A – Freshman rushing record (Robert had 1,126 rushing yards on 177 carries, breaking the record previously held by Archie Griffin when he gained 867 yards as a freshman in 1972.)

47) D – A.J. Hawk (The number 47 is now retired in honor of Chic Harley.)

48) C – 3 (Tressel was named Coach of the Year in 1991 and 1994 while at Youngstown State and 2002 at OSU.)

49) C – 1970s (91-20-3, .811)

50) C – Fred Morrison (He was named MVP as a fullback after gaining 127 rushing yards on 24 carries in the 1950 Rose Bowl [OSU 17, Cal 14].)

Note: All answers valid as of the end of the 2008 season, unless otherwise indicated in the question itself.

Third Quarter

BUCKEYEOLOGY TRIVIA CHALLENGE

1) How many times has a #1-ranked Ohio State team lost in a bowl game?

   A) 2
   B) 4
   C) 5
   D) 7

2) What is the Ohio State record for most tackles in a single game against Michigan?

   A) 17
   B) 22
   C) 29
   D) 34

3) What year was the first 10-win season at Ohio State?

   A) 1922
   B) 1938
   C) 1942
   D) 1954

4) Which Buckeye head coach has the second highest total wins in team history?

   A) John Cooper
   B) John Wilce
   C) Earl Bruce
   D) Jim Tressel

Third Quarter

5) What was Ohio State's all-time largest margin of victory in a bowl game?

- A) 30 points
- B) 34 points
- C) 38 points
- D) 42 points

6) Who holds the OSU career record for receiving yards?

- A) Dee Miller
- B) Michael Jenkins
- C) Bobby Olive
- D) Joey Galloway

7) Which of the following Ohio State QBs never threw greater than 20 touchdown passes in a single season?

- A) Bobby Hoying
- B) Troy Smith
- C) Joe Germaine
- D) Art Schlichter

8) How many combined kickoffs and punts did the Buckeyes return for touchdowns in 2008?

- A) 1
- B) 2
- C) 3
- D) 5

9) Who is the only Ohio State player to kick 10 extra points in a single game?

A) Josh Jackson
B) Vlade Janakievski
C) Tom Klaban
D) Vic Janowicz

10) What season did Buckeye players receive the most honors?

A) 1993
B) 1995
C) 1998
D) 2002

11) Which is not an Ohio State single-game record set in the 1950 Snow Bowl against Michigan?

A) Most Punts
B) Lowest Total Offense
C) Fewest Rushing Yards
D) Fumbles

12) How many of the Buckeyes' games did Joe Germaine pass for greater than 300 yards in 1998?

A) 2
B) 4
C) 6
D) 7

13) Who is the only Ohio State linebacker to lead the team in sacks for a single season?

    A) James Laurinaitis
    B) Chris Spielman
    C) Andy Katzenmoyer
    D) Na'il Diggs

14) Which Buckeye has the most interceptions in a single game against Michigan?

    A) Chris Gamble
    B) Fred Bruney
    C) Antoine Winfield
    D) Ted Provost

15) Which OSU coach has the best overall winning percentage (minimum 3 seasons)?

    A) Jim Tressel
    B) Woody Hayes
    C) John Cooper
    D) Earl Bruce

16) What is the highest total offense for OSU against Michigan?

    A) 512 yards
    B) 538 yards
    C) 581 yards
    D) 602 yards

17) Who was the most recent Buckeye to record greater than 100 solo tackles in a single season?

    A)   Tom Cousineau
    B)   Chris Spielman
    C)   A.J. Hawk
    D)   Pepper Johnson

18) Did Ohio State gain greater than 2,500 rushing yards as a team in 2008?

    A)   Yes
    B)   No

19) When was the last time the season-leading passer for Ohio State had fewer than 1,000 yards passing?

    A)   1955
    B)   1962
    C)   1976
    D)   1983

20) How many Ohio State players have won Rose Bowl MVP?

    A)   1
    B)   5
    C)   7
    D)   9

Third Quarter 3-Point Questions

21) Which of the following players did not lead the Buckeyes in rushing and receiving in the same year?

   A) Keith Byars
   B) Archie Griffin
   C) Ron Springs
   D) Hopalong Cassady

22) Who is the only OSU head coach also named consensus All-American as a Buckeye?

   A) Wes Fesler
   B) Paul Bixler
   C) Carroll Widdoes
   D) Harry Vaughn

23) Chic Harley is the only non-Heisman winning player to have his jersey retired by Ohio State.

   A) True
   B) False

24) Who was the first consensus All-American wide receiver at Ohio State?

   A) Doug Donley
   B) Cris Carter
   C) Joey Galloway
   D) Terry Glenn

25) Ohio State has been ranked #1 in the AP Poll more weeks than any other school.

A) True
B) False

26) Which Buckeye had the longest reception in 2008?

A) Brian Robiskie
B) Ray Small
C) Brian Hartline
D) Dan Herron

27) What is the only Ohio State bowl victory in which an Ohio State player did not receive MVP?

A) 1981 Liberty Bowl
B) 1983 Fiesta Bowl
C) 1993 Holiday Bowl
D) 1995 Citrus Bowl

28) Who was the most recent receiver to lead the Buckeyes in scoring?

A) David Boston
B) Cris Carter
C) Ted Ginn Jr.
D) Joey Galloway

29) How many Buckeyes have been named consensus All-American more than once?

    A) 9
    B) 12
    C) 16
    D) 21

30) What was the combined winning percentage of coaches who lasted one season or less at Ohio State?

    A) .468
    B) .489
    C) .506
    D) .543

31) OSU had a fourth-down conversion percentage greater than 50 percent in 2008.

    A) True
    B) False

32) What is Ohio State's longest drought between bowl games since 1950?

    A) 5 years
    B) 7 years
    C) 10 years
    D) 12 years

Third Quarter   *3-Point Questions*

33) How much does Ohio State's Victory Bell weigh?

    A) 1,862 lbs.
    B) 2,420 lbs.
    C) 2,908 lbs.
    D) 3,309 lbs.

34) How did Ohio State score its first points in the 2009 Fiesta Bowl against Texas?

    A) Touchdown Pass
    B) Kickoff Return
    C) Touchdown Run
    D) Field Goal

35) Have the Buckeyes ever had two 1,000-yard rushers in the same season?

    A) Yes
    B) No

36) How many consecutive regular-season 100-yard games did Archie Griffin have as a Buckeye?

    A) 14
    B) 19
    C) 26
    D) 31

37) How many Buckeyes were drafted in the 2004 NFL Draft?

    A) 8
    B) 11
    C) 14
    D) 16

38) Who is the only Buckeye to lead the team in passing and rushing in the same year?

    A) Troy Smith
    B) Les Horvath
    C) Vic Janowicz
    D) Mike Tomczak

39) What were Ohio State's original chosen colors?

    A) Blue and Gold
    B) Orange and Black
    C) Green and White
    D) Crimson and White

40) When was the last time Ohio State's season-leading rusher gained fewer than 500 yards?

    A) 1963
    B) 1980
    C) 1991
    D) 2004

Third Quarter   *3-Point Questions*

41) In 1892, to what team did Ohio State lose twice?

    A) Wabash
    B) Denison
    C) Oberlin
    D) Kenyon

42) Including the 2009 draft, how many Ohio State players have been drafted in the first round of the NFL Draft?

    A) 59
    B) 66
    C) 68
    D) 71

43) What position did OSU's Coach Tressel play in college?

    A) Defensive Back
    B) Receiver
    C) Punter
    D) Quarterback

44) Who coached Ohio State in its first Big Ten season?

    A) Alexander Lilly
    B) Charles Widdoes
    C) Woody Hayes
    D) John Wilce

45) What are the most points OSU scored in a single game in 2008?

    A)   39 points
    B)   42 points
    C)   45 points
    D)   48 points

46) Did Craig Krenzel out rush the entire Miami Hurricane team in the 2002 National Championship game?

    A)   Yes
    B)   No

47) Where did the Buckeyes play before Ohio Stadium?

    A)   Cooper Stadium
    B)   Ohio Field
    C)   Vets Memorial
    D)   Nationwide Arena

48) What is Ohio State's longest drought between Big Ten Championships?

    A)   6 years
    B)   12 years
    C)   14 years
    D)   18 years

49) Is Archie Griffin the only Buckeye to start in four Rose Bowls?

    A) Yes
    B) No

50) What are the Buckeyes' most consecutive bowl losses?

    A) 2
    B) 4
    C) 7
    D) 9

Third Quarter Buckeye Cool Fact

The Buckeyes finished 8-0-1 overall, including 6-0 in conference play in 1961. Having won the Big Ten, Ohio State should have represented the conference in the Rose Bowl. However, there was no official contract in place between the Rose Bowl and the Big Ten due to a scandal that had taken place in the Pac-10. Therefore, school officials were given authorization to approve or disapprove the team's appearance in the bowl game. Ohio State faculty felt too much emphasis was being placed on the football team. In order to balance the importance of academics with athletics, they voted not to allow the football team to play in the Rose Bowl. A rally was organized to voice disapproval of the school's decision. Ironically the athletic department's own Woody Hayes would appear at the rally in firm support of the school's decision, telling those who arrived to return home. Woody was already well known for the importance he personally placed on academics. Ultimately he would provide not only the academic balance the faculty sought, but civic balance the community needed as well.

Third Quarter Answer Key

1) B – 4 (Top ranked Ohio State lost to #11 UCLA in the 1976 Rose Bowl, #3 Southern Cal in the 1980 Rose Bowl, #2 Florida in the 2006 BCS Championship Game, and #2 LSU in the 2007 BCS Championship Game.)

2) C – 29 tackles (Chris Spielman in 1986; OSU 26, Michigan 24)

3) D – 1954 (10-0)

4) A – John Cooper (111 wins from 1988-2000)

5) A – 30 points (OSU beat BYU 47-17 in the1982 Holiday Bowl.)

6) B – Michael Jenkins (He gained 2,898 yards on 165 receptions from 2000-03.)

7) D – Art Schlichter (Art's highest season total was 17 in 1981, Germaine's was 25 in 1998, Hoying's was 29 in 1995, and Smith's was 31 in 2006.)

8) B – 2 (Ray Small returned a punt 69 yards against Ohio and Etienne returned a blocked punt 20 yards against Purdue.)

9) D – Vic Janowicz (He accomplished this versus Iowa in 1950 [OSU 83, Iowa 21].)

10) B – 1995 (Eddie George: Doak Walker, Heisman, Walter Camp, and Maxwell; Terry Glenn: Biletnikoff; and Orlando Pace: Outland)

11) D – Fumbles (This record was set in 1934 versus Indiana. In the 1950 Snow Bowl Ohio State punted 21 times, managed only 41 yards total offense, and 16 yards rushing [all team records].)

12) D – 7 (The next highest number of 300+ yard passing games in one season is 2.)

13) C – Andy Katzenmoyer (In 1996 Andy led the team with 12 sacks for -74 yards.)

14) B – Fred Bruney (1952, 3 interceptions)

15) A – Jim Tressel (He has led the Buckeyes to a record of 83-19 since 2001 for a .813 winning percentage.)

16) A – 512 yards (OSU set this record in 1961 [OSU 50, MICH 20].)

17) B – Chris Spielman (Chris recorded 105 solo tackles in 1986. Tom Cousineau is the only other Buckeye to record greater than 100 solo tackles in a season. He achieved this in 1976 with 102 tackles and again in 1978 with 142 solo tackles.)

18) A – Yes (The Buckeyes gained 2,502 rushing yards on 540 attempts for a 4.6 yard-per-rush average.)

19) C – 1976 (Jim Pacenta led the team with 404 yards passing.)

20) B – 5 (Fred Morrison [1950], Dave Leggett [1955], Rex Kern [1969] Cornelius Greene [1974], and Joe Germaine [1997])

21) B – Archie Griffin (In 1984 Keith Byars led the team in receiving with 479 yards and 1,764 yards rushing; in 1977 Ron Springs led the team with 90 yards receiving and 1,166 yards rushing; and in 1954 Hopalong Cassady led the team with 137 yards receiving and 609 yards rushing.)

22) A – Wes Fesler (Coached the Buckeyes from 1947-50 and was named consensus All-American in 1928-30 as an end.)

23) B – False (The Heisman award was first given in 1935. Chic played in 1916-17 and 1919. Chic's jersey [#47] was retired in 2005. Bill Willis also had his jersey [#99] retired in 2007.)

24) B – Cris Carter (He was named consensus All-American in 1986 after gaining 1,127 receiving yards with 11 touchdowns.)

25) B – False (The Buckeyes and Oklahoma are tied for second at 86 weeks. Notre Dame has held the top spot for 89 weeks.)

26) C – Brian Hartline (He had a 56-yard reception from Terrelle Pryor against Michigan State.)

27) A – 1981 Liberty Bowl (Navy running back Eddie Meyers was named MVP [OSU 31, Navy 28].)

28) D – Joey Galloway (He led the Buckeyes in scoring with 78 points in 1993.)

29) C – 16 (James Laurinaitis was the most recent multiple All-American recipient at Ohio State [2006-08].)

30) D – .543 (They had a combined record of 27-22-9.)

31) B – False (The Buckeyes converted 4 of 9 fourth-down attempts for a success rate of .444.)

32) C – 10 years (No bowl appearances between 1959-1968)

33) B – 2,420 lbs.

34) D – Field Goal (Aaron Pettrey kicked a 51-yard field goal with 7:28 left in the first quarter to give OSU a 3-0 lead [OSU 21, Texas 24].)

35) A – Yes (Pete Johnson had 1,059 yards and Archie Griffin had 1,450 yards in 1975.)

36) D – 31 (Archie holds the NCAA record for consecutive regular-season 100-yard games.)

37) C – 14 (This broke the NCAA record set by Miami in the 1975 draft.)

38) B – Les Horvath (In 1944 Les led the team in rushing with 924 yards and passing with 344 yards.)

39) B – Orange and Black (It was changed to scarlet and gray after discovering Princeton already had orange and black.)

40) D – 2004 (Lydell Ross led the Buckeyes in rushing with only 475 total yards on 117 carries.)

41) C – Oberlin (The Buckeyes lost to the Yeomen by a combined score of 4-90 [OSU 4, Oberlin 40; OSU 0, Oberlin 50].)

42) C – 68 (Second only to Southern Cal's 73 first-round picks)

43) D – Quarterback (Tressel was All-Conference in 1974 while playing for Baldwin Wallace.)

44) D – John Wilce (He led OSU to a 1-2 record the first year in the conference.)

45) C – 45 points (The Buckeyes beat Michigan State 45-7 and Northwestern 45-10.)

46) A – Yes (Krenzel had 81 rushing yards while the Hurricanes had a total of 65 rushing yards.)

47) B – Ohio Field (Home of the Buckeyes from 1898 to 1921. It had an original seating capacity of 5,000.)

48) C – 14 years (No conference championships between 1921-1934)

49) A – Yes (Archie started in four consecutive Rose Bowls from 1973-76.)

50) B – 4 (On two occasions: bowl games following the 1977-80 seasons and 1989-92 seasons)

Note: All answers valid as of the end of the 2008 season, unless otherwise indicated in the question itself.

Fourth Quarter *4-Point Questions*

1) How many Ohio State players are in the College Football Hall of Fame for multiple positions?

    A) 0
    B) 1
    C) 2
    D) 4

2) When was the last time the Buckeyes failed to score a touchdown in a game?

    A) 1996
    B) 2000
    C) 2005
    D) 2008

3) What was the first year over 100,000 fans attended an Ohio State-Michigan game?

    A) 1957
    B) 1961
    C) 1965
    D) 1969

4) Has Ohio State ever had greater than two players gain 100+ rushing yards in the same game?

    A) Yes
    B) No

Fourth Quarter *4-Point Questions*

5) Which Buckeye kicked the most field goals in a single game against Michigan?

 A) Mike Nugent
 B) Tom Klaban
 C) Vlade Janakievski
 D) Josh Jackson

6) Who was OSU's opponent for the Ohio Stadium dedication game?

 A) Notre Dame
 B) Michigan
 C) Indiana
 D) Illinois

7) What are the most consecutive bowl games in which Ohio State has appeared?

 A) 5
 B) 7
 C) 10
 D) 12

8) How many Ohio State coaches are in the College Football Hall of Fame?

 A) 2
 B) 3
 C) 5
 D) 6

Fourth Quarter *4-Point Questions*

9) Who is the only Buckeye to be named Super Bowl MVP?

    A)   Eddie George
    B)   Tom Tupa
    C)   Santonio Holmes
    D)   Jim Lachey

10) What former head coach compiled a 2-0 record against Ohio State?

    A)   Howard Jones
    B)   John Eckstorm
    C)   Carl Widdoes
    D)   Jack Ryder

11) What is the name of the location where Ohio State All-Americans have a tree planted in their honor?

    A)   Buckeye Grove
    B)   All-American Path
    C)   Football Grove
    D)   Harper's Grove

12) How many times did a Buckeye rush for 100 yards or more in a single game in 2008?

    A)   7
    B)   9
    C)   11
    D)   13

Fourth Quarter *4-Point Questions*

13) Did OSU lead the Big Ten in red zone offense in 2008?

A) Yes
B) No

14) Who holds the Ohio State single season rushing record?

A) Archie Griffin
B) Raymont Harris
C) Eddie George
D) Michael Wiley

15) When was the last season the Buckeyes were shutout?

A) 1971
B) 1987
C) 1993
D) 2001

16) Who holds the records for rushing touchdowns in a
    game, season, and career at Ohio State?

A) Pete Johnson
B) Archie Griffin
C) Eddie George
D) Tim Spencer

Fourth Quarter *4-Point Questions*

17) Who was the Buckeyes' first African-American All-American?

   A) Pete Johnson
   B) Steve Tovar
   C) Bill Willis
   D) Jack Tatum

18) Who did OSU play in their longest game in history?

   A) Miami
   B) NC State
   C) Marshall
   D) Michigan

19) Did Vic Janowicz gain 1,000 career rushing yards for the Buckeyes?

   A) Yes
   B) No

20) Who is the only Buckeye quarterback to lead the team in passing for four years?

   A) Craig Krenzel
   B) Cornelius Greene
   C) Rex Kern
   D) Art Schlichter

Fourth Quarter *4-Point Questions*

21) How many all-time head coaches has Ohio State had?

  A) 17
  B) 19
  C) 21
  D) 23

22) What is Ohio State's largest margin of victory against Michigan?

  A) 25
  B) 32
  C) 38
  D) 44

23) Which coach has the second best winning percentage at Ohio State (minimum three seasons)?

  A) John Eckstorm
  B) Earl Bruce
  C) Wes Fesler
  D) John Cooper

24) Has Ohio State played every Pac-10 team at least once?

  A) Yes
  B) No

Fourth Quarter *4-Point Questions*

25) What is the name of the junior honorary society that represents Ohio State in presenting the Illibuck trophy?

- A) Bucket and Dipper
- B) Bucks and Nuts
- C) Scarlet Club
- D) Varsity Club

26) Against which BCS Conference does Ohio State have the worst winning percentage?

- A) ACC
- B) Pac-10
- C) Big East
- D) SEC

27) What instrument did the first person to dot the "i" play?

- A) Drums
- B) Trumpet
- C) Trombone
- D) Oboe

28) How many Buckeye coaches have won National Coach of the Year while at Ohio State?

- A) 1
- B) 3
- C) 4
- D) 6

Fourth Quarter *4-Point Questions*

29) What decade did Ohio State have its worst winning percentage?

    A) 1890s
    B) 1910s
    C) 1920s
    D) 1950s

30) What season did the Buckeyes win their 800th game?

    A) 2003
    B) 2005
    C) 2007
    D) 2008

31) How many Ohio State players are in the College Football Hall of Fame?

    A) 21
    B) 23
    C) 26
    D) 29

32) Who was the first non-Pac-10 opponent for Ohio State in a bowl game?

    A) BYU
    B) Colorado
    C) Boston College
    D) Alabama

Fourth Quarter *4-Point Questions*

33) When was the last time the Buckeyes gave up a safety?

    A) 1975
    B) 1986
    C) 1994
    D) 2007

34) What was the worst defeat Ohio State suffered in a bowl game?

    A) 26 points
    B) 29 points
    C) 32 points
    D) 35 points

35) Who holds OSU's Rose Bowl rushing record?

    A) Pepe Pearson
    B) Jim Otis
    C) Archie Griffin
    D) Keith Byars

36) How many times has Ohio State appeared in the Orange, Sugar, Fiesta, and Rose Bowls combined?

    A) 17
    B) 19
    C) 21
    D) 23

Fourth Quarter *4-Point Questions*

37) How many Ohio State players have won the Outland Trophy?

    A) 2
    B) 3
    C) 4
    D) 5

38) Who was the most recent consensus All-American lineman at Ohio State?

    A) Rob Murphy
    B) Nick Mangold
    C) Korey Stringer
    D) Orlando Pace

39) How many Ohio State linebackers have won a bowl MVP?

    A) 2
    B) 3
    C) 4
    D) 5

40) Every 300+ yard passing game by a Buckeye quarterback has taken place since 1980.

    A) True
    B) False

Fourth Quarter   *4-Point Questions*

41) Which Ohio State Heisman Trophy winner was drafted highest in the NFL Draft?

    A) Eddie George
    B) Vic Janowicz
    C) Archie Griffin
    D) Hopalong Cassady

42) How many OSU players have won the Lombardi Award?

    A) 2
    B) 3
    C) 4
    D) 5

43) Which Ohio State player received the most individual awards in a single year?

    A) Archie Griffin
    B) Eddie George
    C) David Boston
    D) Orlando Pace

44) What was the best winning percentage of an Ohio State head coach who lasted one season or less?

    A) .600
    B) .700
    C) .750
    D) .825

BUCKEYEOLOGY TRIVIA CHALLENGE

45) When was the last time the Buckeyes shut out an opponent?

    A) 1985
    B) 1996
    C) 2002
    D) 2006

46) Did any Ohio State opponent rush for greater than 250 yards against the Buckeyes in 2008?

    A) Yes
    B) No

47) How many OSU players are in the Rose Bowl Hall of Fame?

    A) 2
    B) 4
    C) 6
    D) 8

48) What is the Ohio State record for most consecutive wins without a tie?

    A) 18
    B) 20
    C) 22
    D) 24

49) What is the Ohio State record for consecutive Big Ten wins?

- A) 15
- B) 17
- C) 20
- D) 23

50) Which Buckeye coach was quoted as saying "Now we have The Best Damn Team in the Land!"?

- A) Jim Tressel
- B) Earl Bruce
- C) Woody Hayes
- D) John Cooper

Fourth Quarter Buckeye Cool Fact

Chic Harley was the first of many outstanding players to put on a Buckeye uniform. Ohio State's record was 21-1-1 during his three seasons. He became their first three-time consensus All-American [1916-17 and 1919]. Later he became a member of the first class inducted into the College Football Hall of Fame. Then in 1950 he and Jim Thorpe were named first-team halfbacks to the Associated Press's All-Star college football team of the first half of the 20th Century. One of his biggest honors may be having his name forever associated with Ohio Stadium. Due to the overwhelming excitement he brought to Ohio State football, a new stadium was needed to accommodate all the fans. For this reason, many say plans were drawn up for the construction of Ohio Stadium, which is often referred to as "The House that Harley Built". Chic returned to Ohio Stadium in 1949 for a tribute in his honor. The marching band altered Script Ohio to Script Chic. This remains the only time the formation has ever been altered.

Fourth Quarter Answer Key

1) C – 2 (Warren Amling was inducted in 1984 as a guard and defensive tackle. Les Horvath was inducted in 1969 as a quarterback and halfback.)

2) D – 2008 (Ohio State lost 3-35 to Southern Cal.)

3) A – 1957 (101,001 fans packed Michigan Stadium [OSU 31, MICH 14].)

4) A – Yes (OSU has had 3 separate players rush for 100+ yards in the same game three different times; 1956 versus Indiana, 1970 versus Duke, and 1989 at Northwestern.)

5) B – Tom Klaban (He kicked four field goals in 1974 to score all of Ohio State's points in a win against the Wolverines [OSU 12, MICH 10].)

6) B – Michigan (This was the third game of the season [OSU 0, MICH 19].)

7) C – 10 (The Buckeyes went to a bowl game each year from 1989-98.)

8) D – 6 (Howard Jones [1951], John Wilce [1954], Francis Schmidt [1971], Woody Hayes [1983], Earl Bruce [2002], and John Cooper [2008])

9) C – Santonio Holmes (He was named MVP of Super Bowl XLIII after gaining 131 yards on nine receptions and catching the go-ahead touchdown for the Pittsburgh Steelers.)

10) A – Howard Jones (Coached Southern Cal to regular-season victories in 1937-38)

11) A – Buckeye Grove (This tradition began in 1934. The grove is located just south of the stadium.)

12) B – 9 (Chris Wells had eight 100-yard games. Terrelle Pryor had one.)

13) A – Yes (The Buckeyes scored on 26 of 26 red-zone series scoring 18 touchdowns and eight field goals.)

14) C – Eddie George [He gained 1,927 yards on 328 carries in 1995.)

15) C – 1993 (The Buckeyes fell 0-28 to Michigan.)

16) A – Pete Johnson (5 rushing touchdowns in a game [tied with Keith Byars], 25 rushing touchdowns in 1975, and 56 rushing touchdowns for his career from 1973-76)

17) C – Bill Willis (This Buckeye great was honored in 2007 by having his jersey [#99] retired. Bill is in the Ohio High School, College Football, and Pro Football Halls of Fame. He is also recognized as the first black player to start in the NFL.)

18) B – NC State (OSU played three overtimes against NC State in 2003 for a total game time of 4:17 [OSU 44, NC State 38].)

19) B – No (He gained 802 career rushing yards from 1949-51 [112 yards in 1949, 314 in 1950, and 376 in 1951].)

20) D – Art Schlichter (He led the team in 1978 [1,250 yards], 1979 [1,816 yards], 1980 [1,930 yards], and 1981 [2,551 yards].)

21) D – 23

22) C – 38 (OSU beat Michigan 38-0 in 1935.)

23) A – John Eckstorm (He led the Buckeyes to a 22-4-3 record from 1899-2001 for a .810 winning percentage.)

24) A – Yes (OSU has an overall record of 50-24-2, with winning records against every team except for Southern Cal and Stanford.)

25) A – Bucket and Dipper (The Illinois junior honorary society is Atius-Sachem.)

26) D – SEC (The Buckeyes' all-time record against the SEC is 7-11-2 [.400], ACC is 13-7 [.650], Pac-10 is 50-24-2 [.671], Big East is 43-10-1 [.806], and Big 12 is 28-5-1 [.838].)

27) B – Trumpet (Trumpet player John Brungart dotted the "i" all three times during the 1936 season.)

28) C – 4 (Carroll Widdoes [1944], Woody Hayes [1957], Earl Bruce [1979], and Jim Tressel [2002])

29) A – 1890s (OSU had a record of 39-40-4 during the decade for a .494 winning percentage.)

30) D – 2008 (Ohio State's 800th win came against Ohio on Sept. 6, 2008. The Buckeyes' all-time record is 808-306-53 for a .715 winning percentage.)

31) A – 21 (Rex Kern was the last inducted in 2007.)

32) B – Colorado (The Buckeyes beat the Buffaloes 27-10 in the 1977 Orange Bowl.)

33) D – 2007 (The Buckeyes gave up a safety to the Akron Zips for their only score [OSU 20, Akron 2].)

34) B – 29 points (OSU lost 6-35 to Alabama in the1978 Sugar Bowl.)

35) C – Archie Griffin (He had 22 carries for 149 yards and one touchdown in the 1974 Rose Bowl.)

36) D – 23 (Orange 1, Sugar 3, Fiesta 6, and Rose 13 [BCS Championship games played since 2006 are not included in these numbers].)

37) C – 4 (Orlando Pace [1996], John Hicks [1973], Jim Stillwagon [1970], and Jim Parker [1956])

38) A – Rob Murphy (He was named consensus All-American as an offensive guard in 1998.)

39) C – 4 (Rowland Tatum [1984 Fiesta], Larry Kolic [1985 Citrus], Chris Spielman [1987 Cotton], and Lorenzo Styles [1993 Holiday])

40) B – False (John Borton passed for 312 yards in 1952 against Washington St. This is the only 300-yard passing game prior to 1980.)

41) D – Hopalong Cassady (Detroit, 2nd pick overall in 1956)

42) D – 5 (A.J. Hawk [2005], Orlando Pace [1995-96], Chris Spielman [1987], John Hicks [1973], and Jim Stillwagon [1970])

43) B – Eddie George (He was awarded the Doak Walker, Heisman, Walter Camp, and Maxwell in 1995.)

44) C – .750 (Howard Jones led OSU to a 6-1-3 record in 1910.)

45) D – 2006 (OSU beat Minnesota 44-0.)

46) B – No (The most rushing yards allowed by the Buckeyes was 214 yards by Illinois. Ohio State held opponents to an average of 119.4 rushing yards per game and 3.5 yards per carry.)

47) B – 4 (Archie Griffin [1990], Rex Kern [1991], Fred Morrison [1993], and Pete Johnson [2007]; Woody Hayes was inducted as a coach in 1989.)

48) C – 22 (1967-69, and again from 2002-03)

49) C – 20 (Set from 2005-07, this is also a Big Ten record.)

50) A – Jim Tressel (Quoted during the post game interview following the 2002 National Championship game; "We've always had The Best Damn Band in the Land, now we have The Best Damn Team in the Land!")

Note: All answers valid as of the end of the 2008 season, unless otherwise indicated in the question itself.

Overtime Bonus *4-Point Questions*

1) Which coach has the second longest coaching tenure at Ohio State?

   A) John Cooper
   B) Jim Tressel
   C) Earl Bruce
   D) John Wilce

2) What is the Buckeyes' longest winning streak in the Ohio State-Michigan series?

   A) 3
   B) 5
   C) 6
   D) 7

3) Which Ohio State running back was not picked in the first round of the NFL Draft?

   A) Eddie George
   B) Keith Byars
   C) Robert Smith
   D) Jeff Graham

4) How many times did the Buckeyes have a player gain 100 or more receiving yards in a single game in 2008?

   A) 1
   B) 3
   C) 5
   D) 7

Overtime Bonus *4-Point Questions*

5) How many yards was the Buckeyes' longest rush in 2008?

    A) 47 yards
    B) 53 yards
    C) 59 yards
    D) 68 yards

6) What year did Ohio State make a 31-point comeback against Minnesota?

    A) 1973
    B) 1981
    C) 1989
    D) 1993

7) How many times has OSU finished last in the Big Ten?

    A) 1
    B) 4
    C) 7
    D) 10

8) How many Ohio State players had over 100 tackles in 2008?

    A) 0
    B) 1
    C) 2
    D) 4

Overtime Bonus *4-Point Questions*

9) What is Ohio State's lowest final AP Poll ranking after beginning number one in the first poll?

    A) 5th
    B) 10th
    C) 15th
    D) 20th

10) What are the most points ever scored by Ohio State in a single game?

    A) 68
    B) 98
    C) 128
    D) 158

Overtime Bonus Answer Key

1) D – John Wilce (16 years, 1913-28)

2) B – 5 (OSU won every meeting from 2004-08.)

3) D – Jeff Graham (2nd round pick by Pittsburgh in 1991)

4) A – 1 (Brian Robiskie gained 116 yards on five catches against Texas in the Fiesta Bowl.)

5) C – 59 yards (Chris Wells had a 59-yard rush against Michigan.)

6) C – 1989 (Ohio State rallied from 31-0 to win 43-37. This tied a then NCAA record for biggest comeback.)

7) A – 1 (OSU has only finished last in the Big Ten one time, in 1947.)

8) B – 1 (James Laurinaitis had 130 total tackles [52 solo and 78 assisted].)

9) C – 15th (In 1980 OSU started the season number one, finished 9-3 ranked 15th in the AP Poll.)

10) C – 128 (OSU scored 128 in the 1916 game against Oberlin as part of its first Big Ten Championship season, and first undefeated/untied season.)

Note: All answers valid as of the end of the 2008 season, unless otherwise indicated in the question itself.

Player / Team Score Sheet

BUCKEYEOLOGY TRIVIA CHALLENGE

Name:_____

First Quarter			Second Quarter			Third Quarter			Fourth Quarter			Overtime	
1	26		1	26		1	26		1	26		1	
2	27		2	27		2	27		2	27		2	
3	28		3	28		3	28		3	28		3	
4	29		4	29		4	29		4	29		4	
5	30		5	30		5	30		5	30		5	
6	31		6	31		6	31		6	31		6	
7	32		7	32		7	32		7	32		7	
8	33		8	33		8	33		8	33		8	
9	34		9	34		9	34		9	34		9	
10	35		10	35		10	35		10	35		10	
11	36		11	36		11	36		11	36			
12	37		12	37		12	37		12	37			
13	38		13	38		13	38		13	38			
14	39		14	39		14	39		14	39			
15	40		15	40		15	40		15	40			
16	41		16	41		16	41		16	41			
17	42		17	42		17	42		17	42			
18	43		18	43		18	43		18	43			
19	44		19	44		19	44		19	44			
20	45		20	45		20	45		20	45			
21	46		21	46		21	46		21	46			
22	47		22	47		22	47		22	47			
23	48		23	48		23	48		23	48			
24	49		24	49		24	49		24	49			
25	50		25	50		25	50		25	50			
___ x 1 =___			___ x 2 =___			___ x 3 =___			___ x 4 =___			___ x 4 =___	

Multiply total number correct by point value/quarter to calculate totals for each quarter.

Add total of all quarters below.

Total Points:_____

Thank you for playing Buckeyeology Trivia Challenge.

Additional score sheets are available at:
www.TriviaGameBooks.com

85

Player / Team Score Sheet

BUCKEYEOLOGY TRIVIA CHALLENGE

Name:_____

First Quarter		Second Quarter		Third Quarter		Fourth Quarter		Overtime
1	26	1	26	1	26	1	26	1
2	27	2	27	2	27	2	27	2
3	28	3	28	3	28	3	28	3
4	29	4	29	4	29	4	29	4
5	30	5	30	5	30	5	30	5
6	31	6	31	6	31	6	31	6
7	32	7	32	7	32	7	32	7
8	33	8	33	8	33	8	33	8
9	34	9	34	9	34	9	34	9
10	35	10	35	10	35	10	35	10
11	36	11	36	11	36	11	36	
12	37	12	37	12	37	12	37	
13	38	13	38	13	38	13	38	
14	39	14	39	14	39	14	39	
15	40	15	40	15	40	15	40	
16	41	16	41	16	41	16	41	
17	42	17	42	17	42	17	42	
18	43	18	43	18	43	18	43	
19	44	19	44	19	44	19	44	
20	45	20	45	20	45	20	45	
21	46	21	46	21	46	21	46	
22	47	22	47	22	47	22	47	
23	48	23	48	23	48	23	48	
24	49	24	49	24	49	24	49	
25	50	25	50	25	50	25	50	

| ___ x 1 = ___ | ___ x 2 = ___ | ___ x 3 = ___ | ___ x 4 = ___ | ___ x 4 = ___ |

Multiply total number correct by point value/quarter to calculate totals for each quarter.

Add total of all quarters below.

Total Points:_____

Thank you for playing Buckeyeology Trivia Challenge.

Additional score sheets are available at:
www.TriviaGameBooks.com

87